Soul Comfort for Cat Lovers

Coping wisdom for
heart and soul after the
loss of a beloved feline

Liz Eastwood

Soul Comfort for Cat Lovers: Coping wisdom for heart and soul after the loss of a beloved feline

Cover and book design by Adina Cucicov, Flamingo Designs

ISBN-13: 978-0615739120
ISBN-10: 0615739121

Dedicated to anyone who's ever
had a feline soul mate.

And to Bastet.

Table of Contents

• v •

PART 2
Finding Comfort in Wonder
Allowing the possibility that death is not the end

PART 3
Conclusion: Emerging Whole After Loss

Introduction

Know You Are Not Alone

*"Her death was as important to me
as the death of anyone I have ever loved.
It was the death of a great soul."*
Author Phillip Schreibman,
My Cat Saved My Life

When the world doesn't seem to understand what you're going through, you may question if it's normal to feel devastated over the loss of your feline companion. I assure you that it is, and you'll find plenty of validation in this book.

"One of the worst [things people said] was the comment, 'It's always hard when a pet passes away.' I was enraged

by the reference to my cats as mere 'pets.' They were part of my family, and I did not lose 'pets,' I lost FAMILY."
Sharon K, cat guardian

A 2011 Harris poll found that at least 91% of cat households think of their cat as a member of the family. The same applies to dogs. And, as we'll discuss, often the bond is so deep that people find themselves confessing that the loss of their animal companion has hit them at least as hard as any loss they've had before.

That means this kind of grief is serious. It means your grief process deserves far more care and respect than the world may be giving it.

Even if you've experienced a difficult loss before, grief can be inexplicably unique each time. If losing your beloved cat companion has hit you particularly hard, the good news is that there are many people who have experienced what you are going through and were able to get through it with their hearts intact—even if they doubted they could. I know, I'm one of those people who doubted I could.

Everything in this book is here to ease the suffering of this loss you may feel so alone in—whether your cat has died or has gone missing for so long that you've had to give up hope.

Let this book be your friend as you find your way through the haze of grief. You will get to the other side and you can live wholeheartedly after this loss. Your feline friend would want nothing less for you.

The Story Behind This Book: A Cat Named Bastet

The best birthday gift I ever received was a little black kitten named Bastet. I named her after the Egyptian cat goddess. With this name, I imagined she'd be incredibly poised and majestic, gracing our home with her knowing calm.

Well, she was more spunky-wild than poised-calm. As a kitten, her tiny claws made a Velcro sound as she ran across the couch, which she did constantly. And she'd flash into the sideways crab jump when she was surprised. As an adult, her tail would puff out like a squirrel when she was particularly happy about a toy or seeing you after a long time apart.

She'd tire people out playing fetch with hair ties and spongy balls. She usually greeted me at the door when I got home, often saying hello in the window as we walked up (even when there was already food in her dish).

She was so attached to being a part of my morning journaling routine that she'd race me to the couch as I approached it with my tea and journal in hand. She usually assumed her spot one second before I did.

This ritual with Bastet was meaningful because it was the most peaceful and spiritual time of my day. It was when I would drop into a meditative space and the best answers to my life's questions would come to me. I often felt that Bastet's presence was an influence on this special state of mind.

To this day, I still imagine—or suspect—her presence is there when I journal in the morning.

When Bastet was barely twelve, she was diagnosed with high-grade intestinal lymphoma—the kind of cancer for which all vets give a short-term death prognosis.

No, no, no, no! This could not happen to her.

But it did. And so one of the hardest times in my life began: me determined to save her in spite of the prognosis, me feeling responsible for the cancer, and then ...

... me not saving her and feeling like all the sunlight had been packed up and removed from the world.

Yet people were still driving to work, chatting about TV shows, and ordering cheesecake for dessert. Didn't these people realize the sun had disappeared? I could no longer comprehend the day-to-day world.

You might think that with the meditation and spiritual study I'd undertaken, a background in the health and wellness field, and forty years of life lessons and other losses behind me, I would not have been brought to my knees by the death of my cat companion. But I was.

I discovered that when we are reeling from the loss of an intimate, loving, loyal friend, we can be too shocked by the concept of death itself, too depleted by sorrow, and too muddled in our thinking to have the energy and clarity to raise our own spirits and revive our own soul.

And so began my journey into what to do about all that. When I went looking for help with my suffering, resources I found on animal companion loss were helpful at times, but tended to feel dog oriented.

Grief and loss may be the hardest thing we face in this life, and they are particularly excruciating when we feel others do not understand.

When the grief was very fresh, nearly anything anyone said to make me feel better only made me feel worse. I needed support, but it wasn't worth risking the pain of someone trivializing the loss of my cat friend.

When I finally got to the other side of the agony of loss, having learned a great deal, I found that I longed to somehow help other cat lovers on this lonely path of the soul. A few years later, I began writing this book.

Taking on the Big Mystery: Finding Comfort in Wonder

The fear that death is an empty ending is often at the core of our deepest pain. When we have a special companion die, we long to know whether their spirit lives on and if there is any possibility we can still be connected or meet again.

I discovered that when a death hits you very hard, the big questions about death itself sometimes make it twice as hard to recover from grief.

In fact, some people say you need to work through your feelings about the mystery of death before you can fully recover from grief. That was my experience. This is why I wanted to write about the most soulful of the soul comforts: the possibility of the continuation of your loved one's spirit—and your connection to that spirit—after death.

So I tackle this subject in Part 2. I explore it spiritually and open-mindedly, but without applying any dogma or belief system. For the sake of the left side of your brain, I even bring in some encouraging scientific perspectives.

But first, in Part 1, you'll find the most helpful wisdom and practices I gathered on my own loss journey and in my research and interviews for this book.

Trust Your Instincts

Please read just what your heart is drawn to in this book, and read the chapters in whatever order calls to you. That will be your best path to restoring your spirit and finding peace.

Part I

Coping with the Loss of Your Feline Friend

Wisdom for mind, body, and spirit

Chapter 1

How Long Should This Be Taking?

You may have asked yourself: How long does this take? How long will this pain last?

I remember being stunned that the tears kept pouring out. I'd think, *"Well, there, that's it. I've clearly gotten it all out now,"* and yet, to my surprise, there the tears would be again the next day or next week. Grief can also cause a feeling of depression to hang around longer than you'd expect.

The Grief Timeline

You've probably heard of the general stages of grief: Denial; Anger; Bargaining; Depression; Acceptance. But it turns out that we jump around within those stages—and you can't force a linear path through them.

While we can't skip grief, I can tell you that:

- The first three months after your loved one dies or goes missing are usually the hardest
- There's a reason many cultures have an official grieving period of a year
- There are ways to go through this so that it's less devastating and less of a struggle

Animal companion grief counselor, Jill Goodfriend, RN, LCSW, echoed this timeframe when I asked her opinion. She said that, in her personal and professional experience, *"It takes a year to get through all the holidays, the birthdays, the celebrations ... and then you say 'I got through the first year, I think I'm gonna make it.'"*

She emphasized that it's not that you feel despair for 365 days, but that there are waves of sadness that come and go as we move through the seasons.

But you don't have to experience paralyzing depression for months and months. And you can emerge whole, with the ability to be happy again. If you work with the suggestions in this book that resonate for you, I am confident that your grief will shift from deep misery to a more loving "at peace" feeling.

"I have found the paradox, that if you love until it hurts, there can be no more hurt, only more love."
Mother Teresa

You can eventually find wellbeing. You find it by not letting the feelings fester and corrode inside you, but by actually feeling them so they can move on. We'll explore gentle ways to do this in this book.

In spite of experiencing greater grief than I had ever known, and feeling terrible for not preventing Bastet's cancer and saving her from it, the ability to embrace and enjoy life again came back to me in less than a year because of many of the practices I talk about in this book.

At the one-year anniversary of Bastet's death, I was dreading what misery might take me in its grip again. Yet, when my partner, Robert, and I did our private grave-side ceremony to honor her that day, I found that I felt more love and peace than pain.

When the next day came, and the next, I found that I felt stronger and more committed to live in the way that I think she wants me to live. I felt more resolved to allow my positive experiences with her to be a guiding force in my life.

Ever since that one-year anniversary, I've been able to feel more joy than pain when I think of her.

It's Different Every Time

Each loss experience has its own timetable in your heart.

You will have feelings when you're ready for them. You will grow when you're ready to grow. You'll do new things when you're ready to do new things.

You will seek support when you're ready to seek support. You will find what you need when you need it—you've already begun to.

But trusting the timing of your heart requires you to ignore those who don't understand what you're going through right now, which is what we get serious about in the next chapter.

Resources and Further Reading

- **The Five Stages of Loss and Grief**, Julie Axelrod, PsychCentral.com

Chapter 2

Learning to Ignore Everyone Who Doesn't Get It

"Until one has loved an animal, a part of one's soul remains unawakened."
Anatole France

As I mentioned earlier, you are hereby allowed to consider your cat a family member, as wise grief counselors and 91% of cat guardians already do. After all, our connections with animal friends are often more constant and reliably loving than our connections with humans (which are, alas, more complicated).

The fact that our bond with a cat companion is "uncomplicated" does not mean it isn't stunningly deep.

One of the first blog posts I wrote was about feline soul mates. Though the readership was still small at the time, it struck a chord and attracted a lot of comments. Here are some comments people have left on that post:

> *"My beautiful cat ... crossed the rainbow bridge yesterday evening after a long battle with oral cancer. He has been my rock and light for 14 years; there are no words to describe the pain the sorrow and the emptiness I feel!"*

> *"I could not deal with any more platitudes from those who have no connection with the animals they share their lives with or who suggested I replace him with another."*

> *"My connection to [him] was unexplainable and his death has left me devastated."*

The Relationship Others Can't See

Our friendships with our cats can be very intimate and loyal, yet our cats can seem rather invisible to the rest of the world—even to our good friends.

Others rarely see the cat we know.

This is partly because of the private nature of cats, the way they come out of their shell when others aren't around. Plus, people aren't likely to see you at the park with them, or walking down the street with them. Even when our animated, loving cat meets our friends in our home, our cat may act more distracted or shy than usual.

People also don't see how constant and close our connection is with our cats. They don't see our cat greeting us when we come home every day or giving us that slow love-blink (the cat smile). They don't see the extended eye contact communication we have, or hear them chirrup back when we ask them questions, or see them comfort us when we are suffering.

Others can't see the fabric of the routines we develop together either, as captured in these lines Phillip Schreibman wrote about his cat, Alice, in his beautiful gem of a book, *My Cat Saved My Life*:

> *"Each night she got on the bed and lay beside me, leaning her weight against my leg ... We lay there together in the darkness while the city traffic continued to roar outside ... My mind was roaring too: with all the angers and sorrow and fears that had plagued me during the day. But something in her presence made a stillness settle on the room."*

A lovely woman named Christina wrote to me about her cat, Karma, who had recently passed away after 18 years together:

"One day after a nightshift I counted that when I came home she gave me 27 Eskimo kisses on the nose!!! What man would do that? She was always beside me with cuddles, chirrups, love— spiritual warmth.

So many times she would be at the other end of the room and I would feel such love, I'd look around and she would be there! She'd smile and blink!

Other times I'd hold her and fill up with love everywhere.

She was so full of love, especially as she neared the end of her life. As she went between both worlds, she let me know she really loved me.

I'm destitute without her by my side."

So yes, some people don't get it. But there are countless people who do. Someday, those who don't get it may be lucky enough to form a bond with a feline friend like yours, and then they will understand. Until then, listen only to the people who get it.

Meanwhile, your healing journey begins with understanding that your feelings in grief are normal, as you'll see in the next chapter.

- Learning to Ignore Everyone Who Doesn't Get It •

Resources and Further Reading
- *My Cat Saved My Life* by Phillip Schreibman
- "The feline soul mate—do you have one too?," Liz Eastwood, NaturalCatCareBlog.com

Chapter 3

Understanding What Feelings Are Normal at This Time

M any people have said that the death of an animal companion affected them *at least* as intensely as the passing of human loved ones.

It's a phenomenon we don't speak of too often, but when I asked grief counselor Jill Goodfriend, RN, LCSW if she'd seen this, she said "almost everyone" reports this to her.

Then I discovered an article in the *Washington Post* that referenced multiple studies on this topic. The title of the article said it all: *"The death of pet can hurt as much as the loss of a relative."*

So we now know that what we're dealing with here is the *big* kind of grief. We can no longer trivialize it.

We have to acknowledge the full range of responses known to grief experts.

Feelings of Guilt

Because our cats seem so dependent on us, guilt is one of the most common feelings when they die. We may put a great deal of blame upon ourselves.

Moira Anderson Allen's excellent article on this topic at pet-loss.net points out the irony that it's the most sensitive and careful caretakers who feel the most guilt. Those who don't care much wouldn't even have these feelings.

I had all kinds of guilt. I lamented not giving Bastet a better life and was pained over everything I might have done differently to prevent and reverse the cancer.

After Bastet got sick, I so obsessively and intensely fought for her life that her vet later wrote that my devotion was "unparalleled"—yet I still felt guilty.

But here's what I realize now: With all my heart, I loved my cat and wanted her to be happy and healthy. I'm sure the same applies to you.

And, there are many assumptions about how to help our cats be healthy and happy, and some of these assumptions turn out to be wrong. There is so much we still just don't know.

But none of that is your fault.

Yes, cats can get sick, die, or go missing partly because of mistakes that we, a vet, or someone close to us made. But the essential thing to realize is that accidents and mistakes are exactly that: completely unintentional—the opposite of what you intended.

With all your heart, you always did the best you knew how to do with the time, resources, and information you had. And I believe that at an instinctive level your cat knows this.

A Sense of Unreality and Other Common Reactions to Loss

It helps to know the common emotions you and your family may experience while grieving. Remember, you're dealing with the loss of family member, so you need to know that it's normal to have any of the following reactions.

EMOTIONAL	MENTAL	BEHAVIORAL	SPIRITUAL	PHYSICAL
Anger	Absent minded	Avoidance	Anger at the Divine	Blood pressure changes
Anxiety	Confusion	Carrying objects that have memories	Feeling closer to or more distant from the Divine	Blurred vision
Depression	Denial	Crying	Exploring new dimensions of faith	Chest pain
Despair	Detachment	Depersonalization	Looking for meaning and "Why?"	Diarrhea or constipation
Disorganization	Disbelief	Dreams of deceased	Reassessing values and beliefs	Difficulty breathing
Emptiness	Disorganized thinking	Isolation	Seeking or questioning faith	Digestive problems
Fear	Insecurity	Overactivity	Visions	Dizziness
Frustration	Lack of concentration	Restlessness	Visitations	Fatigue
Guilt	Loss of control	Searching		Headaches
Hate	Lower self-esteem	Social withdrawal		Lack of energy
Helplessness	Preoccupation	Visiting places with memories		Lowered immune system
Hopelessness	Sense of presence			Nausea
Loneliness	Sense of unreality			Numbness
Numbness	Think you're going crazy			Sensitivity to light
Overwhelm	Yearning			Sleep disturbance
Panic				Stomach ache
Reconciliation				Tightness in throat
Regret				Weight loss or gain
Relief				
Remorse				
Resentment				
Sadness				
Self-pity				
Shock				

Source: Journal of the American Osteopathic Association, JAOA.org

Shock or Numbness in the Face of Unexpected Loss

If your loss was sudden and unexpected, if you felt forced to make life-and-death decisions without time to fully process them, or if you experienced multiple losses at once, your grief may be particularly overwhelming.

Sometimes it's so overwhelming that it starts with a protective sense of numbness, unreality, or confusion. This is natural because it's almost impossible to process the weight of an unexpected loss quickly.

> *"It takes time for the brain and the heart to process a loss, to move from shock, disbelief and denial (healthy initial responses) to accepting the loss into one's daily life and functioning fully again."*
> **Jill Goodfriend, RN, LCSW**

Allow your psyche to take the time it needs. I recommend being gentle with yourself and taking up some of the suggestions in the chapter on replenishing your coping reserves.

If you feel stuck, a good pet loss counselor can also help you with healing from the shock or thawing out the numbness. You'll find recommendations for finding one in a later chapter.

When You're Troubled by Upsetting Memories or Images

When there has been a traumatizing experience, such as witnessing an accident, your trauma has to be processed before your loss can be fully processed. Feeling haunted by upsetting memories or images you witnessed is a symptom of that kind of trauma. If this is something you are struggling with, consider finding a pet loss counselor with EMDR (Eye Movement Desensitization and Reprocessing) training or other training for dealing with trauma. See the chapter on finding support for more information.

Positive Feelings Arising Out of Grief

It's also possible to have feelings on the opposite side of the spectrum after a loss.

Some of these feelings can come as a reaction to the end of a long illness and struggle, but many of them are also related, I believe, to your own healing and spiritual awakening:

- love
- sense of feeling empowered, stronger
- gratitude and appreciation
- deep connection
- relief
- generosity

- deeper sense of meaning and purpose
- clearer priorities

As I grew stronger, sometimes I would fluctuate between these positive feelings and the difficult ones.

I noticed that the more I allowed the experience of grief to be completely about my love for the friend I lost, the more my heart opened, and the more often I'd experience a "present moment-ness" that would contain these positive feelings that have a spiritual essence to them.

Resources and Further Reading

- "Breaking the Power of Guilt," Moira Anderson Allen, pet-loss.net
- "Coping with unexpected loss: a personal journey," Ingrid King, ConsciousCat.net
- "The death of a pet can hurt as much as the death of a relative," Joe Yonan, *Washington Post, March 26, 2012*

Chapter 4

Giving Sorrow
the Space to Transform

*"When we resist emotions, they're forced into
unconscious expression, giving them greater
power over us and leaving us feeling even more
out of control, stuck, and afraid in our grief."*
Cath Duncan, Creative Grief Educator and Coach at
RememberingforGood.com and GriefCoachingCertification.com

While loving memories and awareness of the physical absence of your cat may last, the most painful feelings are temporary when given proper space and attention.

On the subject of grieving, author Phillip Schreibman wrote, *"It's alright to cry every day if we feel like it. It is as important as laughing ... We kill ourselves if we stop it."* This wisdom in Schreibman's book, *My Cat Saved My Life*, was particularly powerful because the reader knows he earned it the hard way. Schreibman had discovered what stuck, unexpressed grief can do to your own life force.

When he described that trapped, depressed state, I recognized so much of the modern world in it. But we don't have to end up in that place where a heart broken turns metallic, miserable, or resigned. We *can* make sure our feelings don't get stuck inside where they can drain our life force forever. That means the feelings need room, which is why so much of this book is about ways to give them that healthy space to transform: it's key to processing grief and emerging as a whole person.

Sorrow Needs Space to Transform

Some people become stuck in depression a year or more after the loss of their cat because they resisted crying and even avoided looking at photos of their cat after the loss. By cutting themselves off from the feelings, they could not progress on their grief journey. As a result, they languished in a depression. (If this sounds like you, don't despair; you are progressing on your path now just by choosing to read this book.)

I like to imagine giving the sad feelings lots of space—the whole universe—to move. Only then can they move on. Put another way, my friend's mother said the best advice she received after losing her husband was to "steer into her grief." You need to drive through it rather than around it.

While your feelings will follow their own timeline, I can assure you that allowing the feelings to flow when they appear, and honoring them as pure, clean and healthy, gets you to a better place.

In the process, we honor the companion we lost. As a wise visitor to my blog said, *"I am allowing myself to grieve for his loss; he was a loving, affectionate companion for a long time and it would be disrespectful and disloyal to not grieve for him ..."*

It's essential to realize that the tears and the feelings are energies that need to move through you, even if they don't make perfect sense to your thinking mind.

But the Feelings Are So Painful, How Can I Do This?

I know, it's a thousand times easier to say "let your feelings run their course like a river to the sea" than it is to actually feel the pain. So let me share the process that worked for me, which you can adapt in your own way.

First, I suggest you think of the grief you feel as pure, because it is: it comes from the depths of love. Imagine it enveloped in the most honoring space you can imagine, such as a sacred temple for the grieving.

For many people, it helps to let the feelings out in the presence of a caring, close friend or family member. But let's face it, it's a busy world and we don't always have this luxury.

When struck with a crippling sense of grief, I discovered I could at times feel surrounded by a mysterious larger, loving energy. This helped tremendously and it was made stronger by an image that came to me unexpectedly.

One day, not long after Bastet died, I was driving home from work, and was struck by several powerful waves of grief in my chest. Through my tears, I thought: *How am I going to drive safely on this freeway now?*

But then, in my mind's eye, the image of two mysterious gentle beings in a beautiful temple appeared. The best part was that they were catching me as I had the sensation of falling backward into the feelings. In my "mind's ear" I heard them say, "It's okay. Bastet's with us now. She's okay, she's with us." It was incredibly comforting for me.

Unconsciously activating a technique I learned in hypnotherapy training, I touched the lower-middle of my forehead at that moment. You know, that "third eye" space between your eyes. Instinctively, as the days went by, when I would again find myself falling back into the overpowering grief, I would touch that space between my eyes. This would bring up the image of falling back into the arms of those kind beings again. And again I would feel comforted by their paradoxical assertion that all was well. I was still grieving, but somehow it felt easier to *be with* the grief.

There was also a sense in this vision that grief is deeply sacred and that this envisioned temple symbolized the honor in grieving. It was a very affirming, healing feeling.

Is there any "reality" to any of this? Who can know? While all I know for sure is that it calmed me at the core of my being, I believe these symbolic impressions came from a deeper knowing within that we all have.

Techniques for Giving the Feelings Room to Transform

> *"Get into your parked car, roll up the windows, and scream or cry. Sometimes we just need to give ourselves permission to let it out. In our Western culture, we don't 'do death' well in general, and this is especially true after pet loss, which is disenfranchised grief."*
> **Jill Goodfriend, RN, LSCW**

Here are some techniques for tapping into your inner wisdom and giving the feelings room to transform:

1. **When you are in a safe environment and the feelings come up, pause before you push them away.** Experiment with allowing yourself to lean gently into the feelings.

o Your way of expressing your feelings is very individual. It may happen through art or by throwing stones in a river—alone or with others. The important thing is to find the form of expression that works for you.

o When feelings come up, invite a supportive image or phrase to come to you. If none appears, experiment with imagining what that image or phrase would be if it did appear.

o If a comforting image or phrase comes to you, try anchoring it by touching your heart or touching the "third eye" space between your eyes. The next time you are feeling overwhelmed by grief, touch that space again and allow the calming image or phrase to come back to you.

2. **Don't ever judge your emotions,** they are a way of honoring someone you loved and they are the way to heal. When I was able to gently lean into the pain, it was because I realized the root of my grief was a pure love and therefore the feelings could not be wrong. If the feelings came from love, it made no sense to deny them.

3. **Allow the process to open your senses and intuition.** When you are really present to letting the feelings flow through you, your senses and intuition start to expand. This is healing because it makes it possible to explore an ongoing sense of connection to the spirit of the one you lost. Consider being open to a sense of their presence and what they would say to you.

4. **Experiment with adapting at least one of the rituals, ceremonies, or tributes** suggested in this book. These are very effective ways to give your feelings some healthy space for transformation.

5. **If you sense you need more support, consider finding a grief counselor or pet loss support group.** Refer to the chapter on support near the end of this book for help with this.

6. **Give yourself the nourishment, rest, and care grief requires.** You'll discover my best tips on how to do this in the chapter on restoring your coping reserves.

7. **If your family members are grieving too, don't forget to honor their feelings** and support their efforts to honor your cat's memory as well.

   ○ Accept that their grieving process may look very different from yours.
   ○ Don't be afraid to cry in front of your children, and let them know it is okay to express their love in this way.

What To Do When Grief is Inconvenient

For many of us, one of the biggest challenges when we lose a cat companion is facing the work or school environment while the heartbreak and sorrow are still hitting us in crushing waves. Full-time parenting can also make grief feel inconvenient. We may feel disoriented, too, which makes it even harder.

Grief simply doesn't get the space, time, and respect it needs in our culture. So let's talk about what we can do to deal with the challenges presented at this time. I've been there.

In the Beginning When It's All Just Too Much ...

Many of the people you work with would probably understand—more than you know—about what you're going through. However, professional expectations being what they are, you may have to grind through your workdays on grief-hidden autopilot for a while.

If at all possible, and if your heart needs it, take some time off to grieve and process what you are going through. If you are unable to take time off, there are ways to deal with the disabling feelings while the grief is fresh and you can't shelve it for later:

Know that you are not alone in struggling with this situation, and that the hardest-hitting grief is a temporary situation. If you can give yourself private time outside of work to let the feelings flow in a safe place, you will get stronger each day.

With friends in the workplace, if you feel compelled to explain yourself but don't think they'd understand, you could just say that a friend died and you aren't ready to talk about it. They will honor your privacy.

Some days are worse than others, and many people find that a good cry in the restroom or car, or on a walk, needs to happen. Again, know that this is normal and do it when you need to, if you can.

Keep the friend or family member who most understands how this feels on speed dial. If possible, leave the building to talk to them when you need to. A short cry with someone who cares makes a difference.

Something to Try Once You Can At Least Get Through the Day

Some experts advise setting aside time every day to allow all the feelings to be there, while putting some sacredness or ritual around that time.

Again, don't expect to be able to compartmentalize grief in the first week or so, but I do recommend eventually experimenting with a planned time.

The idea is that when grief threatens to overtake you while you are handling important responsibilities, you can remind your grieving self that you will have a special time and space later to allow what's coming up. Just knowing that can sometimes help you through the moment.

What does this special grieving time look like? It can be talking to a friend or grief counselor. Or going to the place in your home that feels most sacred and safe. The bedroom, perhaps. It can be lighting a candle next to a photo of your cat, and then writing in a journal about your feelings. These activities can gently allow the feelings to move through you instead of getting stuck or showing up at the worst times.

A scheduled time for grieving may not always work for you. It didn't work that well for me, especially in the beginning, because the tears and misery were quite a force. As the feelings ebb and flow, you may at times feel surprisingly strong and centered at your planned grieving time. You may not feel like calling grief forth. That's fine, too. Experiment to see what feels right for you.

Another way to help the energy of grief move through you—at a more "convenient" time—is to create something positive out of that energy: a ceremony or tribute to your companion. There are several ideas for how to do this in upcoming chapters.

But first, let's get your self-care in order, because when your coping hormones are depleted (and they probably are at this point), grief is even harder than it needs to be.

Resources and Further Reading

• *Remembering for Good* by Cath Duncan

Chapter 5

Replenishing Your Coping Reserves

Even though I have a background as a wellness and nutrition counselor, I almost made the mistake of not writing this chapter and assuming that you will practice good self-care without me suggesting it.

Then I remembered struggling through a cold/flu and having a friend ask on the phone, "Are you taking those Chinese herbs that help? Are you having soup and tea?"

Such obvious stuff to me, but no, I wasn't doing those things. Why? Because my head was fuzzy and I wasn't thinking and acting wisely through the fog of my illness.

With the depletion and suffering of grief, it's the same. We aren't thinking that clearly. We don't have the energy to step outside ourselves and say, "Now then, here's what you need to do today to take good care of yourself. First, go to the store and ..."

So here and now, I am that friend on the phone. I am here to give voice to your own inner wisdom.

Following just a few bits of such advice will go a long way in strengthening the mental and physical reserves we are born with to help us cope with hard times. Our brain makes coping chemicals, like serotonin and dopamine, that are more powerful than drugs for giving us the resilience we need to cope in challenging times.

So why, then, do we have a hard time coping? Because during emotional stress those coping chemicals are used up fast. The good news is that the following suggestions will help you restore them.

Seven Ways to Improve Your Coping Biochemistry

Regardless of how long it's been since your cat companion died, when you are feeling grief or depression, you need to be doing these kinds of things. Any family members who are grieving with you should be following this self-care wisdom, too.

1. **Be gentle with your sorrow. Rest and cut yourself some slack.** What feels restful to you right now? Staring into space, watching an uplifting film, reading spiritual books? Entertain some ideas and try them out until you find what works. Also, if being at work feels awful right now, take time off if you can.

    If your heart is deeply hurting and the world expects you to keep delivering at 100%, the world is going to have to wait or settle for less. When you're in your freshest grief, you need to take good care of your own heart and needs. And, ask for help from those who love you.

    Look at your to-do list. Anything that is not "life or death" can be dealt with later—it's not as important as respecting the call of your body and soul when grief has side-swiped you.

    If you have young children, ask friends and family to watch them occasionally. Or hire a babysitter. Give yourself quiet time at home alone. And give older children some quiet time as well—it's okay for them to stay home from school for a day or two.

    Undrugged sleep, which allows for REM cycles, is the greatest replenisher of all. And, it's estimated that just lying down and being quiet gives your body about 80% of the rest it gets while sleeping.

So make both sleep and any activity that feels restful a priority. Be gentle with your sorrow.

2. **Connect with those whose presence feels helpful during this time.** Some people are tiring to be around, particularly when you are grieving. Avoid those folks for now. Other company feels good, validating, and comforting. Spend time with people you feel comfortable with, even while grieving.

3. **Take walks, get outside.** The brain chemistry boost of walking, nature, and sunlight are well documented. Do this every day if possible.

4. **Only read and watch what feeds your spirit and respects your soul.** This is a very important step, because we are bombarded with media and the Internet all day and night. When we are depleted, we forget to take control and be selective.

   Do you feel better or worse when you watch the news? Better or worse when you check Facebook? Don't do what makes you feel worse. Instead, choose only healing, uplifting, and restorative things to watch, do, or read.

5. **Choose food that feels nourishing every day.** Food that feels nourishing digests quickly and easily. It leaves your energy feeling even, and you don't feel hungry for at least 3-4 hours afterward. Food that supports your coping chemistry will have protein in it, as our body cannot make chemicals

like serotonin and dopamine without amino acids that are in protein. Also, natural fats are essential to brain chemistry balance and a lack of fat in the diet causes depression. Include in your diet any natural fats you are drawn to, such as nuts and seeds, real butter, coconut oil, avocado oil, and olive oil.

6. **Consider taking B-complex and magnesium for your coping chemistry.** The B vitamins are required for converting amino acids into your brain's coping chemicals, and you burn through B vitamins very quickly during emotional stress and depression. I believe modern culture is generally B-vitamin deficient. Our body does not store B complex, and many B vitamins are destroyed by cooking and processing. Plus, modern living results in less-than-ideal gut health, which means many of us don't absorb and assimilate our B vitamins very well. Supplementing with a high-quality B complex can make a significant difference in mood and energy levels, and magnesium is a heart-protective co-factor for this.

7. **Drink more water and herbal teas.** Hydration is key to wellbeing. Keep a water bottle or large glass of water at your side for most of the day and evening. Calm Tea by Tazo is a personal favorite of mine.

The modern world is oblivious to what you really need right now. It will keep asking you to "listen to me, work for me, buy me, watch me, do for me …"

Ignore that world and let this list of basics be a constant reminder of how to care for yourself when you are down.

Those who love you will ultimately appreciate you taking care of yourself, as will your own body and soul. You will have a lot more to give later if you apply these self-care practices when you need them.

Chapter 6

Using Ritual to Honor Your Cat, Heal, and Feel Connected

"I created a ritual ...The ritual helped me gently ease into accepting her physical absence. I also wanted my memory of our farewell to be sacred and beautiful, and now when I look back, I always see flowers, valentine colors and candle lights surrounding my angel, and the warm gaze of loving friends upon the two of us..."
Akiko, cat guardian

It's never too late after loss—and probably never too early—to do at least one simple ceremony to honor your feline companion.

With ritual or ceremony, you create a little space of beauty and love amid the chaos and suffering of grief. It has a restructuring effect and shifts energy in a powerful way. As I share in this chapter, ceremony and ritual were an important part of my own grief and healing process.

If you aren't sure it will make any difference, it's worth a try—you may be surprised. Often all it takes is a candle, a picture, and sense of sacredness. This chapter has all the information you need.

As Akiko said in the opening quote, you are also creating a new healing memory to look back on, which is much more healthy than making the passing of your loved one into *the-horrible-experience-buried-in-your-psyche-to-avoid-for-all-time.*

Many of us lose all sense of anchoredness during the emotional shock of loss. Ceremony can be a way of regaining centeredness. It's also a beautiful way to feel more complete in saying farewell, thank you, and "I'm open to continuing a connection to your spirit, in whatever way is possible."

Ritual Ideas

When Bastet died, I wished I had already had a simple ceremony planned and written down somewhere, because I was so devastated that coming up with something creative was quite challenging. This is another reason I wanted to create this book. I wanted a resource to make such moments easier for all of us.

Let your honoring ceremonies be as private or inclusive as you want them to be. It can be meaningful to include at least one other person who knew and loved your cat or at least gets what you're going through.

Some people prefer to do something big—even a traditional burial or ceremony with a cat-loving minister or rabbi. But if you instinctively know you want only people who were very close to your feline friend (perhaps only you!), then by all means, do honor that. Grief can be quite a tender time and tears are the way through it. Don't create an environment that will inhibit your feelings.

Simple Ceremonies

For a ritual honoring your cat, here are some ideas that may be helpful when you don't have a lot of time to prepare.

Light a candle. It can give a sense of ceremony to any moment. If you have a picture of your cat, place that next to the candle. If you can put some flowers in a vase there, too, all the better.

Find a reading that resonates for you and read it out loud. See the Appendix at the end of this book for readings you might like. Even if you don't read something out loud for a ceremony, I hope you'll check out the poems I selected for the Appendix in this book. Many people have found them meaningful.

Speak out loud, to your cat's spirit, about what you are thankful for about having had them in your life. This is the simplest meaningful ritual you can do right away.

Place some sort of symbol of your love and appreciation somewhere meaningful, as a gift to your cat's spirit. You might put it next to his or her ashes or a photo, in a special place in your home. The gift symbol could, for example, be a drawing of a heart with your cat's name on it or some wild flowers in a jar.

Allow the tears if they appear. They are healing. If no tears come yet, don't worry about that, either. Grief has its own individual schedule that we cannot force.

Because of the intensity of the moment, it can help to do some sort of ritual as soon as possible after your companion dies, and then you can do something a bit more formal later. This is what we did, as I describe next.

Creating a Ritual When Your Cat is Missing

If your cat has gone missing, and you don't know if you will see them again, it can be hard to know how or when to create a ritual for them. Consider a ritual that doesn't say "goodbye" but instead sends a message of love to them, wherever they may be, and thanks them for the time you were able to share with them thus far.

Ritual Ideas That Take a Little More Time

Here are some other ceremonies that people have found helpful and healing:

Create an altar-type space to honor your cat. This is where you can go to remember your cat and feel an ongoing sense of connection with their spirit. You might put a candle there, photos, a poem, flowers, and perhaps your cat's favorite toys. Consider any spiritual symbols that feel appropriate to you—from St. Francis of Assisi to Buddha to the Egyptian cat goddess, Bastet (or "Bast"). You can find figurines online. I have an altar area on my dresser that is meaningful for me. It has a Bastet figure on it, and I kept photos of my cat there for a full year before moving them to the living room. Whenever I want to feel more connected to her, I light the candle on that altar. If you have older children who are grieving, encourage them to create their own private altar space if they'd like.

Plant a tree in his or her honor. Some people place an engraved stone or sign under the tree (In loving memory or in honor of ...) and you can even bury ashes there. This can become a very sacred space to commune with the spirit of your cat.

Write an interactive communication with your cat. This suggestion comes from Jill Goodfriend, RN, LCSW, who runs pet loss support groups. Write a letter to your cat with your dominant hand and use your non-dominant hand for your cat's response. It may sound silly, but tapping into the non-verbal hemisphere of the brain with your non-dominant hand may reveal some surprising information. Jill says, *"Even when we've had a chance to say goodbye, we frequently have regrets about what we didn't communicate when our beloved pet was still alive."* This feeling of incompleteness can be especially significant if your cat has gone missing and you don't know what happened to them. This technique can be a healing way to work through what feels incomplete. (Some people can practice this kind of interactive writing using only their dominant hand—see what works best for you.)

Write a series of letters or a journal to your feline companion. This can span months or years. One of the first known books about animal communication, written in the 1930s, was called *Letters to Strongheart* by J. Allen Boone. Strongheart was an amazing movie-acting dog, and the man who cared for him had quite an awakening through their friendship. In his grief after Strongheart died, he traveled and wrote letters to Strongheart. Sometimes the letters were about his feelings and memories involving Strongheart, sometimes he told Strongheart about his amusing experiences, and frequently his letters were philosophical and soulful.

Create a poem or piece of art to express your feelings. If you plan to do a grief expression ritual of creating art, it's best to set an end time and have a plan to do something pleasant afterward, like meet a friend. However, if you create a piece of writing or art more as a tribute than raw expression, a time limitation is not so necessary.

My Ceremony Story

My partner in life, Robert, met Bastet about nine years later than I did, but fell in love with her every bit as much as I did.

One evening, when Bastet was ill and not moving around much, Robert called out, "Goodnight Bastet, I love you!" as he was settling into bed. In response, she appeared suddenly from the next room, jumping up to be with him even though she had hardly moved all day. They had developed quite a bond in a few short years.

So in my disorienting grief when Bastet died, I knew that a ceremony was going to be important for helping both of us manage the feelings that were so crushing for us at that time.

Robert said he wouldn't have done something like this on his own, but told me later that he was surprised at what a difference it made.

Because Bastet died naturally at home, her body was with us. We found a large square, shallow box that we placed her body in. Though we planned to do a ceremony for burial the next day, I wanted to make this meaningful, too. Through a downpour of tears, we lit a candle in the room and then placed small gifts and symbols of our love into the burial box:

- Snipped flowers found outside, and rosemary—the herb for remembrance
- A sweet card with a drawing of a black cat and a heart (I had bought it months before, intending to give it to Robert)
- A couple of her favorite toys: a ball and hair tie

Then we each spoke spontaneously of our gratitude for things she had given us.

Yes, it was heart-wrenching, but it was clean and pure and honest. And nothing on earth seemed to matter more at that moment than being present to these feelings in this way.

We weren't ready for burial that day. Instinctively, it seemed to be better to wait a day. For one night we kept her body in the sacred box with the gifts on my own little altar, which is on my dresser in our bedroom.

When Robert and I did our simple burial ceremony, I read some meaningful passages I had found. With tears, we each spoke a more formal goodbye, and placed flowers down.

For me, it didn't exactly feel like goodbye. For months after she died, I still felt she was near me. I would find myself speaking to her, in my head, without really thinking about it very consciously. It just felt natural. After living with her for so long I had become accustomed to a sense of constant communication between us. This sense of being able to silently talk to her continued for a long while after she died. It's still there at times to this day.

The Power of Rituals As the Year Unfolds

"You have to experience the absence in every season of the year. I finally understood the custom among my people of the year-long mourning period, the Yortzeit. Each change of weather brings different sensory memories of when you last lived through that season."
Phillip Schreibman

As the year ahead unfolds, we are bound to find ourselves thinking things like *"Oh, first winter without her ... oh, he used to love to watch the butterflies come out in spring ... oh, this time last year ..."*

This is one reason why, as Akiko said in the opening quote for this chapter, having a ceremonial way to honor your cat and gradually let go of his physical presence over time can be extremely helpful.

Many older cultures do certain rituals over the course of a year, with special attention to the one-year anniversary of a loved one's passing. I highly recommend this.

For example, Akiko created her own rituals based on practices from her family's Buddhist traditions. The process consisted of a service, cremation, 49 days of memorial, and a first-anniversary ceremony.

For the first 49 nights, she lit small candles around her apartment in spots she associated with her beloved cat. Akiko said, *"Setting a specific period of time created, for me, a bridge to accepting the space without her presence."*

In another example, I read about a simple grief ritual that consisted of lighting a candle next to a picture of your loved one and then waving an incense or sage stick up, down, left, and right while saying, "I love you, I miss you, I love you, I miss you ..." each time. You can change the words, of course, but this worked for me. I used to do that little ritual fairly regularly in the evenings after Bastet died. I simply did it when I was feeling distressed because it helped me feel better.

On the one-year anniversary of Bastet's death, Robert and I had a ceremony at her grave. As I mentioned in the introduction, I was dreading that day, but the ceremony made it feel better—even special. I put flowers on her grave and we each spoke out loud to her spirit, letting her know how much she meant to us and thanking her again for being in our lives. Simple as it was, it was quite meaningful and healing. It felt like the right thing to do.

In addition to a ceremony, many people find that creating a tribute is a meaningful way to honor their cat and ease the pain of grief. So let's look at some wonderful tributes that have worked well for other cat lovers.

Chapter 7

Creating Something Positive Out of Grief Energy: The Tribute

A tribute is a formal way to honor your cat and channel your grief into something positive.

Creating a tribute can be a ceremony in and of itself, and most people find tributes to be a meaningful way to heal.

For example, you may feel called to give something in your cat's honor to a rescue organization. Or your heart may fill with pride at the idea of having a big canvas wall hanging created from a photo of your dear friend.

Tributes That Felt Right to Other Cat Lovers

In my research for this book, I discovered that several kinds of tributes have been meaningful for cat lovers. See if any of these ideas resonate with you. Resources for many of these options are listed at the end of this chapter.

Making a donation to an animal welfare organization like the Humane Society or a feline rescue group. Some people donate food and toys to a shelter in their cat's name. Some people have even set up a fund to finance a feline welfare organization after they die.

Sponsoring a rescued cat. Some cat rescue sanctuaries, like Cat House on the Kings (cathouseonthekings.com), let you go online and choose a cat to sponsor with periodic donations.

Commissioning a painting (or sculpture) of your cat. One woman who had a beautiful big painting of her cat on her wall said the sight of it comforted her every day.

Having a canvas-frame picture created from a photo. You could choose a favorite photo and have it enlarged and printed on a canvas frame, like a big painting. This service may be available at a local photo shop, or you can find it online through services like CanvasOnDemand.com and AllPopArt.com.

Commissioning or engraving jewelry. Some people like to have jewelry, like a charm bracelet, engraved with their cat's name and a heart or paw print, so they can keep the tribute close to them at all times. There is also jewelry that has a small space inside where your loved one's ashes can be kept.

Fostering a cat who needs a home. If you feel ready and called to do this, ask about fostering programs at your local shelter.

Putting a photo of your cat in a frame. A nice frame with a beautiful photo of their friend is something many people love to keep in their home.

Create a piece of art, writing, or poem that honors your cat. What you create can be small and private. Or, you may be inspired to make it big and share it with others who will benefit from it, as Jackson Galaxy did when he wrote his inspiring and moving book, *Cat Daddy: What the World's Most Incorrigible Cat Taught Me About Life, Love, and Coming Clean.*

Finally, two ideas from the ritual chapter can also be done as a tribute:

Planting a tree in your cat's honor. You can have your cat's name engraved on a large stone you place under the tree.

Creating a little altar in memory of your cat. If you're the creative, spiritual type, this can be a satisfying way of making something beautiful and comforting out of your grief. People arrange photos of their companion, meaningful spiritual symbols, flowers, candles, and other things of beauty in a small space to form an altar. It often becomes a place where you meditate or feel more connected with your cat's spirit.

Never Underestimate the Tribute of Talk

It takes time to build up to talking. It took us several months before it felt good to mention happy memories of Bastet in conversation in our home. But eventually it became a joy to mention her and I feel like we honor her every time we do so.

When you're ready, let yourself mention good memories of your cat as they come up in conversation. Talk about the things you loved. It's an ongoing tribute to speak of these things with a heart of full of appreciation.

The Memory Scrapbook as Tribute

Personally, I am really happy that I created a book of photos and notes about Bastet. It was a way to put all the pictures and little things I never wanted to forget in one place. Saving the memories while they were still strong was so helpful that I've dedicated the next chapter to this type of tribute.

Resources for Tributes

- Cat sanctuary where you can choose a cat online to sponsor: **CatHouseOnTheKings.com**
- Commissioned portraits: **Bernadette E. Kazmarski** of **The Creative Cat** offers lovely life-like portraits and Vicki Boatright of **BZTat.com** offers unique contemporary pop art and folk art portraits.
- Photo printing on canvases: **CanvasOnDemand.com** and **AllPopArt.com**
- Urns, plaques, engraved stones, and ash-container jewelry: **PerfectMemorials.com**

Chapter 8

Saving Memories
You Don't Want
to Forget

Many people create the tribute of a memorial scrapbook to make sure they don't forget anything that's important to them.

When you choose to keep alive emotionally, and in memory, what you cherished about your cat, you can eventually focus on these good memories and feelings rather than any painful ones from the end of his or her life.

After all, there are so many more good memories than painful ones—it's just that the painful ones are more recent. Having your special scrapbook helps you shift your focus over time to what you most want to remember.

Shortly after Bastet died, I wanted to make sure I didn't forget those little things about her. Here's what I did:

1. I collected and printed every good photo I could find of her.

2. I collected the funny little cartoons Robert had made about her, and other memorabilia like her Humane Society adoption papers.

3. On blank index cards, I wrote down small things I wanted to remember, as they occurred to me. For example:

"She used to sometimes make a funny long, loud sound like the cartoon character Snoopy when she yawned. Her Snoopy yawns always cracked me up."

"Bastet often slept on my stomach or side while I slept at night. I'm a restless sleeper, but I learned to turn slowly—she would adjust her position as I turned and manage to stay on me without falling off! She was quite a big, long cat, so her ability to do this seemed to defy physics."

I looked for a lovely place to put all these memories. After examining dozens of scrapbooks and photo albums at the store, I finally settled on a little silver one that was meant for wedding photos. I chose it for the size, for being able to insert a picture in the cover, and because it had words about love written all over it, including *Love never ends.*

I realize that at first it can be too upsetting to dwell on memories of your companion, but eventually—when it feels right—you will find joy in talking about what you adored. You will like looking at pictures and reminiscing because it's a way of celebrating and honoring your cat.

Chapter 9

Choosing Continued Connection Instead of "Closure"

"You don't have to 'seek closure.' ... pursuing closure often leads to closed-heartedness. It's safe and healthy to remember your lost loved one. Because remembering doesn't have to be painful. Your remembering can be good for you ..."

Cath Duncan, Creative Grief Educator and Coach at RememberingforGood.com and GriefCoachingCertification.com

I love the above words of Cath Duncan. It challenges the pressure you may feel from society to "move on." And, it's so true that remembering your cat companion eventually can feel healthy and happy, rarely painful.

When I talk about choosing continued connection over closure, I'm talking about two different things:

1. The ongoing love and remembering of your friend, which Cath is speaking of in the quote above.

2. A sense that your feline friend continues to be with you on a spiritual level.

Let's explore these ideas, as they are immensely helpful for moving through grief in a healthy way.

Allowing Continued Connection

Don't give into pressures to "get over" your feelings of grief about losing your friend. As we've talked about, the way through grief is to give these feelings the space and time they need.

Science is showing us we are hard-wired for connection and belonging—they are essential to our wellbeing. If we allow ourselves to feel an ongoing sense of connection and belonging with loved ones who have passed before us, we are going to be happier. Many people believe and practice this instinctively in regard to human family members or ancestors. They keep their pictures in prominent places and visit memorial sites with flowers regularly. We can do these kinds of things with our four-legged family members, too.

If you are one of those who had your cat go missing and don't know whether they are still alive, this topic of connection versus closure can be particularly relevant to what you are going through. The practice of allowing a sense of continued connection applies whether or not your friend is still walking this earth.

What does this continued connection look like? Continued connection means remembering your friend with love, and it's also about an ongoing sense of spiritual connection to them.

In both the remembering and the spiritual connection, it looks like many of the things I talk about in this book.

For example, for me it often looks like:

- bringing up good memories of Bastet in conversations with Robert
- lighting a candle near her photo or on a little altar whenever I wish to feel more connected to her
- allowing myself to communicate with her in my mind or write to her in my journal
- having framed photos of her in a special place in my home

Exploring an Ongoing Spiritual Connection

I don't know how much you thought of your cat as able to understand humans, but over the years I've come to believe that our animal friends have a sort of "higher self," or spiritual self, that comprehends human matters more than we know.

Even if our cats don't appear to have a strong grasp of what humans talk about in this dimension, I suspect they are ahead of us in comprehension once they get to the other side.

Let me share an example of an experience I had after Bastet died that made me feel she had entered a space where we could still be connected and communicate.

On the day Bastet died, in my utter grief, misery, and need for a sign from her, I asked her to answer a couple questions through a deck of symbolic cards. These are cards with illustrations symbolizing various qualities. They come with a cheat sheet to help you understand what cards you randomly pull are meant to symbolize.

My first question came from my anguish over failing to save her. I asked her: *How do you see and feel about me now? Do you think I made terrible choices? Do you blame me for your death?*

Now, several cards in this deck of over 70 cards represented answers I would not have wanted. So I was a little worried, but I already felt so terrible that I didn't have anything to lose.

When I do this "question and answer" practice, I usually draw just one card. So after asking Bastet's spirit my question, I shuffled the deck face down for a while and then stopped and cut the cards when I felt the intuition to do so. For me, this intuition is a subtle physical instinct.

When I turned over the card on the top, my eyes filled with tears. The answer card I pulled blindly and randomly from that large deck was **Love.**

I then felt a clear sense that Bastet was saying, *"I see everything you've done for me has been from love and I just think of you with pure love."* It was probably the greatest gift I could've received at that moment!

I then asked her, in her wisdom from the other side: *What should I focus myself on now?*

I asked this because I felt totally lost. For months I had been focused on almost nothing but trying to save her. Now, in my grief and confusion, I didn't see the point of doing anything at all.

After shuffling again, I pulled a face-down card out to let her answer through it. This card symbolized home, happiness, and cultivating and appreciating the place you live in. It was the last thing on my mind, but Robert and I had bought and moved into our first home the year before Bastet got sick.

Enjoy your new home together, I believe she was saying. Focus on what you have together, take this opportunity to cherish home and cultivate love and beauty there. Again, this message felt just right.

Your Own Ways to Experience a Spiritual Connection

Your ways to open an ongoing sense of communication with your loved one may be different from mine.

Experiment with what works in your own belief system—whether it be prayer, quantum physics, or just trusting that when you look out at the ocean at dusk, you feel connected to your feline friend.

Another great way to explore a connection is through the interactive letter writing practice described in the chapter on rituals. Some grief counselors recommend writing to your loved one with your dominant hand and then seeing what comes up intuitively when you respond by writing with your non-dominant hand.

Similarly, you may experience an intuitive connection by experimenting with free writing or "automatic writing." Automatic writing simply involves setting a timer for 10-15 minutes and just writing whatever comes to mind, even if it seems to be nonsense. Just keep the pen moving. Don't think. First, write to your companion for a set time. Then, stop and set the timer again for another automatic writing session where you open to an intuitive response coming through your writing. It can take a few minutes to feel a flow with this, but you may be surprised at the results.

Working With Dreams

Dreams are another way we may experience a sense of spiritual connection with a loved one who has died.

> *"I had a dream about her last night, that she was playing joyfully and was well. I do believe she is trying to tell me that she is fine now, does not feel the horrible pain and will always be with us."*
> **Monika, commenting on my blog post, *"The feline soul mate—do you have one, too?"***

In my grief, I became focused on dreams after Bastet died. It may be because I had read that some people have a beautiful, comforting "dream visit" from their animal companion. This seems to occur after particularly emotionally difficult deaths.

After so many months where I was completely focused on Bastet with cancer, and every tiny symptom of the illness, I longed to see her as healthy and as whole as she had been all her life up until the cancer occurred.

As is common when we lose someone to a long illness, I was having a hard time remembering her as normal and well, and this really bothered me. Plus, of course, I longed to experience her physical presence again, even if only in a dream.

Some people feel that these dreams are actually visits from the spirit of the friend who has passed—the dream realm being the easiest way for them to appear to us. That's a theory I like. Whether it's true or not, the dream can be quite meaningful.

But it can't be rushed.

Be Patient: My Dream Experiences

After a number of weeks of "asking" Bastet to appear, she finally sailed through the corner of my dream screen one night. I didn't even see her face, just her ears, moving presence, and tail. I woke up incredibly happy about that brief view of her looking healthy.

I can't remember exactly how long this first dream took to occur, but it seemed like an eternity.

Then, it was another few months before I got to experience her more fully in a dream.

On reflection, I wonder if these longed-for dreams may have taken so long because it was my time to really think about what death was. Perhaps, if I had a spiritually reassuring "visit" right after she died, I would not have gone through certain feelings, growth, and explorations that I needed to go through.

It wasn't until many months after Bastet died that I finally had a series of dreams where she was fully with me. This series of dreams played out over the course of several months and I still have them once in a while.

In these dreams, Bastet is healthy and happy, and we are always "out in the world" somewhere. I am usually holding her comfortably in my arms, without any fear she could get lost, even though she had always been an indoor cat, confined by my city living.

The dreams are meaningful to me for a couple reasons. I had always wished she could play with me outside, like my childhood cat did, or go to events with me, the way dogs can. I had always had a longing to be able to have her with me even when I was outside the home, as she was one of my best friends.

In these dreams that finally came, we got to be out together in places like a beautiful forest, an art gallery, and a city hotel with Robert.

What a gift these dreams have been! These were settings I would have loved to have experienced with her, if only it could have been safe to do so.

I believe these dreams have another meaning, too: they invite me to entertain the possibility that her spirit is always with me wherever I go.

Inviting Your Cat Into Your Dreams

Regardless of where you believe these kinds of dreams come from—the spirit world or your unconscious—they are usually very helpful and healing. So if you feel drawn to this, then by all means give it a try.

The "dream visit" may appear without you even consciously thinking of it, but if that doesn't happen you can do what I did: Before you drift off to sleep, ask your cat to visit you healthy and whole in the dream world. Optionally, mention any question you'd like answered or any experience you'd like to have with them in the dream world.

If and when the dream happens, be open to a loving message within it.

Another spiritual exploration that can be helpful in times of grief is the experiment I call "Asking a magic question." I describe it in the next chapter.

Chapter 10

Asking a
Magic Question

Many people report that recovering from the pain of their loss got easier as they allowed certain feelings to move them toward positive change and action.

You may find that grief can change you, or your life, for the better when you ask, what I call, "the magic question." A grief breakthrough happened when I started asking Bastet's spirit, and perhaps the Divine Mystery, *"What would you have me do now with all the raw energy of these feelings?"* I wrote this question in my journal.

I sensed the power of all those feelings may yet have some place it wanted to go, something it wanted to do.

After I wrote that question in my journal, I started to get hints of answers coming to me, which I'd just mull over for a while.

Eventually I acted on the ideas, and the result was that I created a blog dedicated to Bastet, natural cat health, and honoring our soul connections with cats. It also set in motion my intention to write this book.

Though it had never occurred to me create these things before, this work has been very satisfying and meaningful.

As I'll share in the last chapter of this book, other positive changes also grew out of letting the feelings move me.

Asking the Question

Like me, you may get a great deal of benefit from asking a question like: *"What would you have me do now with all the energy of these feelings?"* It helps to write it down somewhere.

Who are you asking? That's up to you, of course. I liked asking my beloved cat's spirit. Some people like to ask such questions of their "wise mind" or "inner guidance" or God.

But here's what's most important: have in mind the energy of love itself, regardless of what you call the source of it. Don't ask fear or anger what to do with the feelings you have from grief. Fear and anger's advice will only provide fleeting relief, and likely harm you or someone else in the long run.

In other words, for a true long-term shift in a happier direction, ask this question of Love, which was always at the heart of the connection with your feline friend, and still is.

Chapter 11

Considering the
Right Time to Adopt
Another Cat

In our grief, we often wonder: *"Should I adopt another cat right away? When is it the right time?"*

The Grief Counselor's Cautious Answer

Generally, many grief counselors say you shouldn't adopt another animal friend in the first few weeks after your loss. They say this because it takes time to work through grief before building a bond with a new cat. And because you may ultimately resent the new cat—either for trying to take the place of your previous cat or for not being just like your previous cat!

For the same reason, they say you should avoid calling a new cat by the same name as the old. And, they recommend against trying to find a "look-a-like" cat right away.

My "It Depends" Answer

On one hand, I agree that if we get a new cat within a couple weeks, we do not give our bodies, hearts, and minds time to process the loss in the healthy way. The replacement approach is usually not healthy for you or your new "stand-in" cat.

However, with millions of unadopted cats still dying in shelters each year, saving another cat's life can be a meaningful way of honoring the beloved cat you lost. You just have to do it for the right reasons.

Sharon K. said that she had seven beloved cats die over several years, and each time she felt devastated, yet having to care for her daughter helped her stay "somewhat functional." But then, when the last cat, Tinkerbell, died at age 16, Sharon was completely shattered. The feelings she hadn't been able to fully go into before came flooding in.

Sharon explained how a visit to the shelter was what she needed at that time: *"I could not sit on my couch without sobbing and got very depressed. The thing that helped me was to go to a rescue, sit on the floor and let the next cat that desperately needed me choose me. My darling BamBam climbed right up to my shoulder where Tinkerbell used to spend nearly all her time, and immediately started purring in my ear. She adopted me and I took her home. The thing that helped was the understanding that there is a time and a purpose for every season. My season with those who had passed was over, and there were others who needed the love I have to give."*

You have to do what feels right to you.

If, like Sharon, a new cat clearly chooses you, serendipity may be at work, and I'd trust that. I've certainly heard a number of stories of kittens appearing out of nowhere right after another cat dies.

In my case, after Bastet died, I began longing to adopt another cat after about three weeks of deep grief. Robert didn't think it was a good idea yet. It took several more weeks to convince him.

We adopted Phil and Joel about six weeks after Bastet died. I think it worked out well because I envisioned these new family members as **in addition to**—not as a replacement of—her.

In my heart, Bastet was still with us spiritually, though we were still grieving the loss of her physical presence.

I think this perspective worked well for us. We kept lots of room and love in our hearts and home for the one who had passed away, even as we got to know and appreciate our new cats, Phil and Joel. We allowed them to show us their own personality, quirks, and ways of connecting—we didn't expect them to be Bastet 2 and Bastet 3 so we could skip the pain of losing her.

I was still grieving Bastet even while our home was filled with the happiness and energy of these two new little guys. But I was able to simultaneously love and celebrate their uniqueness while still thinking of Bastet each day.

If You Are Afraid to Adopt Again

Sometimes, rather than adopting too soon, we go the other direction and think we can never bear to love another cat.

That's how Margaret, a cat lover in Pennsylvania, felt. She said that when her first cat, Buddy, died at age 20, *"I was devastated and I never wanted another cat. I didn't want my heart broken again."*

She kept resisting adoption, even as opportunities appeared. But then a cat named Horshak showed up on her couch—literally—one day and she had to give in.

With Horshak, she found out she could love again and survive grief again, too. Something shifted inside her and she began to dedicate herself to caring for the many cats who come through her yard, home, and life.

Today, she says her answer to grief is *"Love again and better yet love many ... All of those that I loved following Buddy are a tribute to the love I received from Buddy. I just know that when I leave, I will have a menagerie waiting for me at the Rainbow Bridge."*

So My Best Advice ...

My best advice is to follow your heart, but keep the following in mind:

Think of any new cat as "in addition to" not "in replacement of" your cat. I liked to imagine Bastet's presence was still there in our home, even picking out the new kittens for us, looking after them, and winking at us through them at times. To me, her presence will always be with us on some level.

Avoid immediately searching for a "replica" of your cat. This is likely to breed disappointment for all involved. Of course, if a cat who happens to look like your other cat truly picks you out, don't fight fate.

Be with your grief in as many healthy ways as you can before, during, and after you adopt another cat. These healthy ways are what many chapters in this book are about.

Let the next cat(s) choose you. Cats know who they belong with. Go to the shelter and see which cat is the most drawn to you. If you feel a place in your heart deeply touched by that particular cat, chances are this one is choosing you. It's hard to go wrong with this approach—it works better than focusing on breed or color.

Chapter 12

Knowing When and How to Get More Support

As we learned earlier, grief symptoms can include "feeling like you're going crazy" and "a sense of unreality," not to mention anxiety, depression, and social withdrawal.

When these things are happening because you lost a feline family member, you may feel very alone and unsupported. You may think no one understands. But there are many people who fully understand and sometimes the best thing you can do is get help through the hardest parts.

Signs You May Need More Support

According to Jill Goodfriend, RN, LCSW, a quick self-test is:

- Am I eating more (or less) than usual; am I suddenly gaining (or losing) excessive weight?
- Am I sleeping poorly; do I have little energy or interest in things?
- Am I missing days at work or school; falling behind?
- Am I using alcohol, drugs, overwork, or other addictive behaviors, to numb the pain?
- Have I become isolated, with no one to talk to about my feelings?
- Do I feel hopeless and want to end things; do I think about joining my beloved cat?

Answering "yes" to one or more of these questions is not uncommon in the early stages of grief, but Jill says that if you are still struggling after several months, especially if you have limited social support or have experienced multiple losses, the grief can turn into depression, in which case professional counseling is indicated.

Whether it's one week or one year—or more—after your loss, if you are suffering from some of these symptoms, you could use some support.

Other signs you could benefit from counseling or a support group:

- You just want to talk with someone who really understands
- You feel you haven't been able to properly process your grief
- You feel stuck in a painful or depressed state

Resources for Finding the Right Support

Regardless of how long it's been since your loss, **if your suffering is threatening your livelihood or life,** get whatever help you can find and afford as soon as possible.

See what's offered through your health insurance or employee assistance program. The best kind of counselor will specialize in grief—particularly pet loss or bereavement.

Local Support and Counseling

The **Association for Pet Loss and Bereavement** site (**APLB.org**) provides easy tools for:

• Finding a local grief counselor
• Finding a local pet loss support group

Once you find the name of a couple of local pet loss counselors, see if you can find any reviews of them online. **Yelp.com** can be helpful for reviews of service providers.

Online Support

The **Association for Pet Loss and Bereavement** site (**APLB.org**) offers pet loss support in a live chat room with a trained moderator. There is no cost for this service.

At the time of this writing, they also have an Anticipatory Grief chat room twice per month for people with pets who have received a terminal diagnosis.

Pet Loss Counseling Available by Phone (and More)

Jill Goodfriend, RN, LCSW—Jill specializes in grief recovery and animal companion loss counseling. She is available for consultation online and by phone, office, or home visit. She facilitates grief support groups in the San Francisco bay area. **JillGoodfriend.com**; Phone: (510) 393-1359

Special Counseling for Those Troubled by Difficult Memories

One technique mentioned earlier, called EMDR, is known to be particularly helpful for healing from traumatizing experiences and images in loss, such as a violent death, a painful illness, or any other memory you find very difficult to cope with.

A couple of months after Bastet died, I was able to get to a better place by working with a bereavement therapist to address a few moments that were so difficult I just couldn't get them out of my head. These were memories I didn't want to burden anyone else with, but she understood and provided a safe space to help my healing along with EMDR.

Feeling haunted by upsetting memories or images is a trauma symptom. If this is something you are struggling with, consider finding a pet loss counselor with EMDR training, or other training that addresses trauma.

See **EMDR.com** for more information.

Part 2

Finding Comfort in Wonder

Allowing the possibility that death is not the end

Chapter 13

Choosing Wonder

Whether we're atheist, agnostic, "spiritual but not religious," or devoutly religious, we can be so shocked by the death of someone close to us that we suddenly aren't sure what we believe anymore.

While some people have had reassuring, mystical experiences during a loved one's death, others have a crisis of disbelief in an afterlife when death strikes close to home. We want to believe something else exists, but find our belief lost in a sea of misery.

And yet, the rest of the time, deep down—if we drop into our hearts and the wordless, non-linear part of our brains—most of us suspect there is some way that a spirit or soul survives after death.

After all, there is an essence, a spirit, of someone that is there and then suddenly "gone" when death happens. Since science still cannot explain what exactly consciousness is, it begs the question: what was this essence, where did it come from, and where did it go?

When my feline soul mate Bastet died, my relationship with her, her illness, and her dying process were all so intense that it was like I became aware of death for the first time.

And. Death. Suddenly. Terrified. Me.

All of a sudden, even hearing about someone else's loss—whether it was the death of an animal or human loved one—struck me with such a sinking in my stomach, created such an ache in my heart, that I could hardly tolerate it.

Death became so much more real, yet made less sense than ever.

I realized I had a couple of choices.

I could either become permanently, tragically disappointed in the universe itself—defaulting to a chronic state of cynical resignation—or I could try to recover the best of me, try to rediscover that sense of wonder and optimism I used to have about the Mystery of Life.

When I chose the latter, I knew it was going to require some time, some research, and some soul searching.

It was going to require staring down death and asking the really hard questions:

- Are you, Death, all there is beyond this daily life?
- If there is a Loving Force in the universe, does it have any of the power I assumed it had?

In short, I was going to have to research books and writings that cynics would dismiss. And, I was going to need to rediscover the pieces of modern physics and science that pointed to something beyond the world we think we know.

Complexity Beyond Our Comprehension

One thing that helps me in difficult times is that I long ago decided that the Mystery, that inexplicable source of Love and Life energy, is vastly more complex and intelligent than we can comprehend.

What makes us think that nothing in the universe could be more intelligent and complex than the human brain?

When something bad happens, rather than assuming that there's a creator out there who is either cruel, slacking off, or totally fictional, I tend to assume there's a lot more going on than meets the eye. I lean toward trusting that all of this probably makes more sense in a complexity beyond our comprehension.

Everywhere you look, there are things that modern science cannot explain. Take the near-death-experience reports, for example: What if they are true? What if when you exit this world, you are greeted by a bigger feeling of love than you can possibly imagine? What if that next place really does feel even more real than this one? What if when you get there it feels so wonderful that you don't want to come back here? Each of these assertions are common threads that show up in near-death-experience research.

If those reports are correct, then it's almost an amusing irony that death—the thing we most fear and fight against all our lives—might turn out to be the best thing that ever happened to us. (I suppose, if there were irrefutable proof of this, there could be more suicide and even carelessness about other people's safety. Maybe that's why it has to be a mystery.)

If you are grieving, let me ask you this: Why give up hope and assume an indifferent universe when you don't really know for sure? Why not look instead for reasons to believe there's more going on than meets the eye?

Why not choose wonder? That's what I take comfort in. If you do, too, the next two chapters of this book are for you.

Chapter 14

Looking at
Experiences of
Connection
After Death

I discovered something interesting while doing research for this
book. Did you know it's been found that one of the most effective ways to heal devastating, paralyzing grief is to experience
an after-death communication with your deceased loved one?
Researcher Dr. Julie Beischel says that it has helped where other
therapy has failed.

> *"There's a lot of evidence that spontaneous or even in-*
> *duced after-death communication has a great effect on*

personal grief. A recent meta-analysis performed at the University of Memphis on 64 studies demonstrated this. ...People who have had a mediumship meeting report some miraculous, instantaneous changes."
Julie Beischel, PhD, in an interview with Dr. Dean Radin on Noetic.org

When I read this I thought: perhaps we are *meant* to embrace the instinct to believe a connection continues beyond death; to trust there is something more after death.

Perhaps that's why I became so intent on learning about near-death experiences and after-death communication when Bastet died.

In this chapter I share some helpful things I came across. These are things that stuck with me and continue to shape my ideas about life and death in a helpful way.

Near-Death Experiences
When I pored over all the information I could find about near-death experiences (NDEs), I was heartened by the following themes that arose across various cultures, studies, and reports:

- A feeling of complete love embracing them on the other side—in the form of a being, a loved one, or an awareness of a presence.
- Being greeted by loved ones who have gone before them.

- A sense that this post-life reality felt more real than the "real life" of their earthly world.
- Feeling so wonderful in this other place, so loved and loving, that they did not want to return to their earthly life.
- Experiencing a "life review" where they felt intensely how others felt in response to things they did or said in their life—all cases where they were either helping or hurting another being.

Not everyone experienced all these things, but the overall patterns were significant, as explained in *Evidence of the Afterlife: The Science of Near-Death Experiences* by Jeffrey Long, M.D. and Paul Perry.

Could all these people just be making stuff up? I was encouraged to believe in NDEs by:

- Similar NDE experiences reported even by people or children who had no exposure yet to other people's NDE reports.
- People who had been blind since birth, who had no concept of sight and therefore could not see in their dreams, had vision in their NDE.
- Stories of NDEers reporting accurate, verified details they could not have seen or heard because they were "dead" on the operating table.
- The fact that the brain is considered scientifically incapable of dreaming during most reported NDEs, and that NDEers say the experience does not resemble a dream.

I also had to know if anyone saw animal friends in an NDE. It took me a while to find some reports of animals in NDEs, but thankfully I did finally see some, and that helped ease my mind.

If you are fascinated and heartened by NDE stories, one of the best accounts I can recommend is a book by Anita Moorjani called *Dying to Be Me*. It will give you a different view of death and life.

Anita's book is quite persuasive, partly because her inexplicable cancer reversal after the NDE is well documented. Dying of cancer, she went to tumor free in such a short amount of time that the rapid breakdown of the cancer cells alone should have killed her. Her body shouldn't have been able to detoxify the dying cells fast enough. She also was able to precisely describe a conversation her husband had with a doctor in a hallway beyond a closed door, when she hadn't even been conscious to hear it in the first place.

When Anita was asked in an August 2012 teleclass whether she thought we would see our animal companions in that after-life realm she visited, she answered, "absolutely." She is confident that our animal friends go to the same place we go, as they are part of the larger consciousness we are all a part of, the consciousness she experienced that does not die.

Anita's book was so personal, her story so convincing, that it continues to ease my fear of death. Now when I hear about a death, I remember Anita's experience, as well as the other reports I read, and imagine that person or animal embraced by love in a world more real than this one. I've found that this thought feels more healing and true than just about any other thought I could have.

After-Death Sightings and Signs

Here's a story that a woman named Charlie shared on my blog about her much-loved cat:

> *"On the day that she died both my boyfriend and I saw her in the shadows on separate occasions. She was in the spot where she had last sat in the garden and watched him dig her grave. When he had finished I went to her grave and I saw her. When I told my boyfriend, he said he had seen her too but hadn't been sure whether or not to tell me. I think she was just letting us know that she was okay. It was an incredible moment. She was an incredible cat."*

In *Cat Body, Cat Mind*, veterinarian and animal behaviorist Dr. Michael W. Fox devotes a whole chapter to documenting reports of spontaneous after-death experiences people have had with cats and dogs who have died.

On his website, DrFoxVet.com, Dr. Fox describes the communications as *"sometimes visual, either as an aura of light or even a clear image of the animal, or are often purely auditory or tactile, as when the deceased animal's footsteps are heard, a cold nose is felt on one's leg, or the deceased cat is felt jumping onto the bed."*

For weeks after Bastet died, I longed for her spirit to appear to me so I could be reassured she was not gone forever. But nothing happened.

Then, months later, after we adopted two kittens, something happened when I least expected it.

I was staying at my parents' home for a night. No cats lived there, though Bastet had once stayed there for six months.

It was the middle of the night, but I had woken. My eyes were open and I was contentedly drowsy. Suddenly I felt a cat jump up to the foot of the bed, walk up the bed stepping lightly on my legs, and curl up next to me.

As this began to fully register, I realized it was impossible since my parents did not have a cat. It occurred to me that this must be Bastet. I got excited—almost nervous—as I squinted in the dark and pulled my arm out from the covers to reach for her. Yet in that instant she was gone.

I lay there thinking about this experience, letting it sink in.

It would be easy to say, "Oh, it was just a dream," but there was not the clear movement between sleeping and waking that dreams have. I haven't experienced anything like it before or since. I was simply there on the bed with my eyes open from beginning to end. So it's a mystery to me.

After-Death Communication Research

Julie Beischel, PhD, of the Windbridge Institute for Applied Research, is a scientist who didn't believe in the possibility of communicating with the dead.

In fact, she hardly knew what a "medium" was until after her father died. In her grief, she discovered a medium and had a reading.

To her surprise, the experience was so profound that she decided to devote herself to the scientific study of the phenomenon of after-death communication. She felt that if communicating with our deceased loved ones is possible, millions of other people could be greatly helped in their grief, but most of them would need some reason to believe in it first.

In an interview with Dr. Dean Radin of Noetic.org, she reported that the Windbridge Institute's "quintuple-blind" scientific experiments, which are performed only with after-death communicators who have passed rigorous screening, are verifying that communication with the deceased appears to be a real phenomenon.

It would take me a whole page to explain how they create these quintuple-blind experiments, and I probably wouldn't explain it correctly. But, suffice to say, they work hard to rule out alternative explanations, including the possibility that the medium is simply reading the mind of the person who lost a loved one.

Speaking of science, next we'll look at some information that suggests there's a lot more to life and death than meets the eye— in a good way!

Resources and Further Reading

- *Cat Body, Cat Mind* by Dr. Michael Fox
- Dr. Michael Fox's website articles, **DrFoxVet.com/info**
- **"Can Mediums Really Talk to the Dead?,"** Julie Beischel, PhD and Dean Radin, PhD, **Noetic.org**
- *Evidence of the Afterlife: The Science of Near-Death Experiences* by Jeffrey Long, M.D., and Paul Perry
- *Dying to Be Me* by Anita Moorjani (Her abbreviated NDE story is also on her website at **AnitaMoorjani.com**)
- *Proof of Heaven: A Neurosurgeon's Journey into the Afterlife* by Eben Alexander M.D.
- **Windbridge Institute for Applied Research: Windbridge.org** has a list of carefully screened after-death communicators (mediums). Some may provide communication with animals.
- **Animal communicator:** Sharon Callahan, **Anaflora.com**, (530) 926-6424. Recommended for the spiritually minded.

Chapter 15

Exploring Science
That Suggests More to
Life and Death

I love the following mind-bending insights because they dem-
onstrate the probability that we—animals, humans, plants—
all exist as part of a field of energy that transcends time and space.

What's even more awe-inspiring is that they speak to the possibility of existence beyond death.

The discoveries that follow imply that our simple human perceptions of life and death and "what you see is all there is" are
ridiculously shortsighted.

Worlds Truly Invisible to the Human Eye

Apparently, our eyes cannot see over 99 percent of the light in the universe. Since light is the way we visually process our world, doesn't this mean there could be whole other worlds operating in front of us to which we have no sensory access?

> *"What we can see is stuff that reflects or emits light with wavelengths in a very narrow band ... from about 750 to 400 nanometres. What we can't see is the rest. That's all matter that reflects or emits light over the other 99.99999999999% of the spectrum. In fact, we're almost blind."*
> **Richard Hammond, Richard Hammond's Invisible Worlds, BBC.com**

Telepathy Research

I take heart in evidence that it's possible to instantly and invisibly communicate at a distance with other beings because it suggests that our consciousness (or our spirit or presence) somehow transcends our physical body, time, and place.

Princeton University's Engineering Anomalies Research lab operated for over 30 years, performing 653 experiments that demonstrated the ability of people to give and receive information at a distance—telepathically.

Other extensive research by that same lab found that our intentions alone—our thoughts—can influence a machine's output. What's up with that?

Rupert Sheldrake, PhD, has studied dogs and cats who know when their human is coming home—even when the human arrives at a random, unplanned time in a different car or by foot. The animal gets up and goes to stand at a window or door before their person arrives—often at the exact moment their person forms the intention to go home.

It's important to note that Sheldrake's phenomenon only seems to happen between animals and people who are very closely bonded, which is why this doesn't work in a lab with random people and animals.

Cleve Backster, a leading lie-detector expert, found that even plants connected to a polygraph registered reactions to human thoughts. Other researchers replicated his findings. He also found plants reacted to their caretakers' intentions (thoughts) at a distance—not just in the same room. Close proximity was not required.

Finally, from the realm of modern physics, we now know that two electrons, once entangled, will always rotate in opposite directions at the exact same time, no matter how far away they are from each other. What does that mean? It means one electron could be in New York and the other in Spain, yet they somehow know what's happening with each other instantly. The thing is, like telepathy, scientists can't explain how this "quantum entanglement" happens. Einstein called it "spooky action at a distance."

Scientific Clues That We Exist Beyond Our Physical Form

How is telepathy possible? Many theorize it's possible because our consciousness is part of a larger field of energy, the same type of field that allows Einstein's "spooky action at a distance" to occur.

Cellular biologist Bruce Lipton, PhD, asserts that our consciousness—our essence—is coming from somewhere else. Therefore, how could it disappear after we die? It doesn't, according to Dr. Lipton.

Let me explain.

When Dr. Lipton recognized through his work that we are operating via information received by a multitude of receptors on our cells, he had an "Aha" moment where he realized *Wait—we're out there—not just in here.*

In his bestselling book, *The Biology of Belief,* Dr. Lipton describes how the cell's scientifically identified "self-receptors" hold the key to someone's identity. For example, we know self-receptors are the key to whether an organ would be a good match for a transplant and that no two beings have 100% self-receptor matches.

Dr. Lipton's stunning point is this: *"The cell's receptors are not the source of its identity but the vehicle by which the 'self' is downloaded ..."* He writes, *"When I fully understood this relationship, I realized that my identity,* **my 'self,' exists in the environment whether my body is here or not.** *"* [emphasis added]

Dr. Lipton explains that it's like a television broadcast: *"... when my physical body dies, the broadcast is still present."*

In a *Sounds True* podcast interview, Dr. Lipton explained that these cell receptors are why (especially with heart and lung transplants), the more tissue transplanted, the more likely the recipient develops characteristics of the donor. He gives the documented example of a girl with a heart transplant who started receiving information in dreams that led the police to find the murderer of her heart donor.

In the Sounds True interview, Dr. Lipton acknowledged what a difference these insights made to him personally, helping him let go of the fear of mortality.

What if Dr. Lipton is recognizing an amazing fact that's hiding in plain sight?

Like the proverbial fish that doesn't know what water is because it knows no other perspective, it's hard even for many scientists to see facts outside of the box of their worldview. Dr. Lipton peered outside of the box to see a perspective that some researchers may not be ready for. But for those of us looking for clues of existence beyond our earthly bodies, his insights offer compelling scientific hints.

Why Close the Door on the Possibility of Something Beyond This Life?

Many embrace the "what you see is all there is" view of the world. Yet the more we know, the more we realize there is so much we don't know and can't see.

So if you can still feel connected to your loved one who has died, why not embrace that? If you, in your heart of hearts, envision being with them again someday, why not allow that possibility? Chances are there's something to it.

Resources and Further Reading

- **"Ten things 'Invisible Worlds' has taught me,"** Richard Hammond, **bbc.co.uk**, Richard Hammond's Invisible Worlds
- Princeton University's Engineering Anomalies Research lab: **Princeton.edu/~pear/**
- *Dogs That Know When Their Owners Are Coming Home: Fully Updated and Revised* by Rupert Sheldrake
- *The Secret Life of Plants: a Fascinating Account of the Physical, Emotional, and Spiritual Relations Between Plants and Man* by Peter Tompkins and Christopher Bird
- **"What Our Cells Can Teach Us,"** Dr. Bruce Lipton interviewed by Tami Simon, Sounds True Insights from the Edge
- *The Biology of Belief: Unleashing the Power of Consciousness, Matter, & Miracles* by Bruce Lipton, PhD and Dr. Bruce Lipton's website: **BruceLipton.com**

Part 3

Conclusion: Emerging Whole After Loss

Chapter 16

Emerging Whole
After Loss

-----

*"... every experience (of loss or gain) is an op-
portunity to learn, to become more resourceful,
to love and to decide what we want to create
with the cards we've been dealt."*
Cath Duncan, Creative Grief Educator and Coach at
RememberingforGood.com and GriefCoachingCertification.com

I think of Bastet stretching with abandon in the sun, bounding
up to me at the door, or excitedly chattering at birds out the
window.

I remember her meowing up at me and turning in place as I sang to her and turned in a circle myself. (Yes, we really used to do that.)

When I think of these things, I know she lived wholeheartedly and she'd want me to do the same.

"Why wouldn't you?" I imagine Bastet would say, *"Why ever not? You have the gift of life. Use it."*

Your Wholehearted Life After Loss

I discovered the concept of "living wholeheartedly after loss" in the wonderful book *Remembering for Good* by Cath Duncan. I recognized it as the shift that eventually occurred for me through grieving Bastet.

Wholeheartedness, described beautifully by Dr. Brené Brown in her book, *The Gifts of Imperfection*, is about loving bravely, *"celebrating a fleeting moment in time,"* and *"fully engaging in a life that doesn't come with guarantees."*

This is the direction we must go in grief. To go in the opposite direction is to create chronic underlying anger or misery.

I have come to realize that, in response to loss, our hearts can actually break open to more love—inside and out.

The Transformation That Came From Leaning Into the Feeling

To my surprise, after the process of losing and fully grieving Bastet, which was one of the most painful things I've ever experienced, I became more clear than ever about what I could handle and what was important to me. Eventually, I even became more optimistic about my life and myself.

How did this happen from something that caused me so much pain?

First, I felt emptied out by the devastating process of trying to save her and then losing her.

From that empty space it was like I was starting over at zero. I felt stripped down to a raw place, but at least it was a place where love ruled. Starting my life over from this place, I could see more clearly what didn't belong, what didn't fit with what mattered to me. I started throwing things out.

The priorities that made sense from that raw-love place became my new guide. I found myself becoming more honest about what was important to me, and making new choices.

As the pain worked its way through me, I felt more tenderness and openhearted love for the important people in my life. I recall calling my mother and offering to spend my tax refund to fund a vacation with her and my stepfather. My stepfather had Parkinson's disease and I wanted us all to enjoy traveling somewhere together before the disease progressed any further. I also recall leaving a voicemail for a dear old friend and spontaneously saying, "You're a wonderful friend and I love you."

I was still suffering, but I was changing for the better.

I stopped trying to be a part of groups where I felt like I had to pretend in order to fit in. I got more honest with some people and set boundaries that required nerve I had never had before.

Even though I tend to be a private, spotlight-shy person, I became brave enough to create a blog with my real name and photo. I did this because in my ongoing passionate dedication to Bastet, I wanted to write about discoveries that could help cats live longer. And I wanted a place to validate the soul connection so many of us feel with the often-misunderstood feline. In the process, I found myself sharing personal stories and feelings that I never would have shared publicly before.

I also realized I had to find my way out of a corporate job that was not at all aligned with the real me.

In these ways, slowly but surely, I changed my life for the better as a response to grief.

How We Can Change Our Lives for the Better Through Grief

To go in the direction of a life we'll love again, I've learned we need to:

- Avoid sidestepping our sorrow for so long that it begins causing us damage from the inside out.
- Avoid closing down from the possibility of wonder and meaningful connection because we've decided Life will always be cruel or indifferent (the "why bother?" worldview).

These responses to any kind of loss—even job loss, injustice, war, or a painful childhood—may be at the core of most of the misery humans feel and inflict on the world.

That means that anything we can do to learn to move through grief in a healthy way is important not just for our own health— it's important for the whole world.

> *"Grief can be a transformational experience ... It's up to each individual whether they'll choose to let grief destroy them, or whether they'll do the challenging and difficult work that will ultimately allow it to be transformed into personal growth and expansion."*
> **Ingrid King, ConsciousCat.net**

I hope you'll take a moment to congratulate yourself on any steps you have taken to heal, including reading this book.

Inspired by the Love of a Cat

Because Bastet's illness was long and dramatic, I spent a great deal of time at her side, dwelling in her space of pure love.

I was surprised to find this space contained an extraordinarily clear view of what mattered. And it gave me that feeling you can have sometimes when you're outdoors at dusk and there's a gold-tinted light gracing the world around you—suddenly all seems blanketed in timelessness.

I believe that being there with her, in the vulnerable state I was in, was how I began to be transformed. That space of purity and wholehearted living was how she lived, and I believe it's how she would have me live now.

Surely your beloved cat lived wholeheartedly and would want the same for you. Let yourself be inspired by imagining what your feline friend would want you to do today, this week, or even with the rest of your life.

"That, we still are"

I thank you for reading this book and giving me the honor of walking part of your sacred journey with you.

May you know that love is stronger than loss and the end is *not* the end.

May your soul continue to guide you on your path of healing and ongoing connection with this feline companion who touched your life so deeply.

And when you think of your cat companion, may you remember the words of Henry Scott Howard, whose poem you'll find in the Appendix: *"Whatever we were to each other—that, we still are."*

Resources and Further Reading

- **SoulComfortForCatLovers.com**, companion site for this book
- *Remembering for Good* by Cath Duncan
- *The Gifts of Imperfection: Let Go of Who You Think You're Supposed to Be and Embrace Who You Are* by Brené Brown, PhD, LMSW

Appendix

Soul Comfort Poems
for Ceremonies

These poems have resonated and given soul comfort to many
of us who have grieved a cat companion or other loved one.

You may want to read at least one of them as part of a ritual for
your feline friend.

In addition to these two poems, I also recommend *Ascension*, by
Colleen Hitchcock, which you can find on her website at col-
leenhitchcock.com/ascension.html.

Do Not Stand at My Grave and Weep
By Mary Elizabeth Frye

Do not stand at my grave and weep.
I am not there; I do not sleep.
I am a thousand winds that blow,
I am the diamond glints on snow,
I am the sunlight on ripened grain,
I am the gentle autumn rain.
When you awaken in the morning's hush
I am the swift uplifting rush
Of quiet birds in circling flight.
I am the soft star-shine at night.
Do not stand at my grave and cry,
I am not there; I did not die.

Death Is Nothing At All
By Henry Scott Howard

Death is nothing at all.
I have only slipped away to the next room.
I am I and you are you.
Whatever we were to each other,
That, we still are.
Call me by my old familiar name.
Speak to me in the easy way
which you always used.
Put no difference into your tone.
Wear no forced air of solemnity or sorrow.
Laugh as we always laughed
at the little jokes we enjoyed together.
Play, smile, think of me. Pray for me.
Let my name be ever the household word
that it always was.
Let it be spoken without effect.
Without the trace of a shadow on it.
Life means all that it ever meant.
It is the same that it ever was.
There is absolute unbroken continuity.
Why should I be out of mind
because I am out of sight?
I am but waiting for you for an interval.
Somewhere. Very near.
Just around the corner.
All is well.

Acknowledgements

A gracious thank you to the pure-hearted people from the Natural Cat Care Blog community who have shared their stories and insights about the love and loss of a beloved cat, including, but not limited to: Sharon K., Monika, Christina, Akiko, Charlie, Margaret Blorigan, Alice Towery, and Amy Sikes.

Heaps of gratitude to Jill Goodfriend, RN, LCSW, a pet loss expert with a deeply personal understanding of the feline-human bond. Jill was generous with her insightful expertise. I also extend sincere thanks to the Mindful Writing teacher, Chris Malcomb, for introducing me to her.

Teresa Brown supported this book through her friendship and thoughtful draft reviews as a cat lover with a thorough understanding of grief. I also thank my family, and my friends Jenna Peterson, Beth Medina, and Heather Sutherland, for being there for me in my grief and for their enthusiasm for this project.

Loving thanks to Robert, who so adored Bastet, and who was a hero through her illness and the grieving afterward. I am blessed to share my life with someone who proves "Real men love cats" and who has been supportive of the challenging changes I've been making in my life.

I am indebted also to the authors I quoted and referenced in this book. Phillip Schriebman, for the beautiful passages he permitted me to share from his book about grief and awakening (every cat-loving spiritual person should discover this wise man); Cath Duncan, for the tremendously helpful words from her elegantly powerful book, *Remembering for Good*; Ingrid King, author and cat-blogging goddess, whose own writing and insights on the cat lover's grief journey are excellent. I also thank Dr. Michael Fox for his research and writings on after-death visits from animal companions.

Let me express gratitude to two other deep thinkers and authors: Anita Moorjani and Bruce Lipton, PhD. They have each written profound and courageous books that helped expand my perceptions of life and death in a lasting way.

Jill Schoff is appreciated for her wise edits and helpful ideas. I was lucky to find a cat-loving editor who understood my intentions so well.

And finally, great praises are due to Sharon Callahan, my feline-loving spiritual mentor, who saw me doing this work before I did.

About the Author

Liz Eastwood is a San Francisco-area writer and blogger. She publishes the popular Natural Cat Care Blog with the tagline *"Never say just a cat."*

Liz studied psychology and English in college, later adding certifications in holistic nutrition and hypnotherapy. She's written how-to guides for Apple Computer, poetry for mystics-at-heart, and courses to help people heal their relationship with food. She's the author of *Natural Flea Control for Cats Made Simple.*

Liz lives with her boyfriend and at least two of the best cats in the world. When she's not writing, hiking, or feeding the cats, she loves to collect experiences and facts that challenge the notion of an indifferent universe.

Bastet

Made in the USA
San Bernardino, CA
09 August 2019